Let's Cook
a Treat

Let's Cook
a Treat

HELEN DREW and ANGELA WILKES

How to use this book

Let's Cook a Treat is full of creative snacks, scrumptious pastries, and special party foods for young children to make at home. Clear step-by-step instructions show you exactly what to do for each recipe. Below are the points to look out for when using this book and a list of things to remember.

Equipment
Illustrated checklists show you which utensils you need to have ready before you start cooking.

The ingredients
The right amount of each ingredient you need is clearly shown in every recipe.

Things to remember

- Do not cook anything unless there is an adult there to help you.

- Read each recipe before you start to make sure you have everything you need.

- Wash your hands and put on an apron before you start cooking.

- Never leave the kitchen while gas or electric burners are turned on.

Increasing the quantities
Each recipe tells you how much the ingredients make. To make more, double or triple the quantities.

Warning
Some recipes contain nuts, which are a choking hazard.

- Whenever you see this symbol in a recipe, always put on oven mitts and ask an adult to help you.

- Be very careful with sharp knives.

- Always turn the oven off after you have finished cooking.

- Put everything away and clean up any mess when you have finished.

DK

A DK PUBLISHING BOOK

U.S. Editor Camela Decaire
Editor Fiona Campbell
Text Designer Caroline Potts
Managing Editor Jane Yorke
Managing Art Editor Chris Scollen
Production David Hyde
Photography Dave King
Illustrators Brian Delf and Coral Mula

First American Edition, 1996
2 4 6 8 10 9 7 5 3

Published in the United States by
DK Publishing, Inc., 95 Madison Avenue,
New York, NY 10016
Visit us on the World Wide Web at http://www.dk.com

A CIP catalog record for this book is available from the Library of Congress.

ISBN 0-7894-1272-1

Color reproduction by Colourscan
Printed and bound in Italy by L.E.G.O.

Contents

MAKING SANDWICHES

With a little imagination, simple sandwiches can be transformed into a real party-time treat. Here you can find out how to make different types of sandwiches and fillings, and on the next page you can see how to decorate and arrange them to create all kinds of fancy sandwiches.

You will need

Butter

Sliced cheese

Slices of ham

Small rolls

Sliced pumpernickel, whole wheat, and white bread

Cream cheese

Sandwich fillings

Chopped hard-cooked eggs mixed with mayonnaise

Grated cheese and carrot mixed with mayonnaise

Mashed tunafish and mayonnaise

Chopped cooked chicken and mayonnaise

COOK'S TOOLS

Cookie cutters

Grater

Fork

Knife

Toothpicks

Plastic wrap or tinfoil

Cutting board

For decoration

Boston lettuce or watercress

Sliced cucumber

Cherry tomatoes cut in half or sliced

Sliced radishes

Carrots peeled and cut into sticks

Filled rolls

Make two cuts in each roll.* Fill the top cut with sandwich filling. Arrange cucumbers, tomatoes, or radishes in the bottom cut.

Sailboat rolls

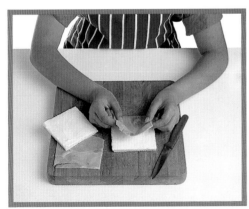

Cut rolls in half.* Spread them with butter and sandwich filling. Make sails from triangles of sliced cheese on toothpicks.**

Pinwheel sandwiches

Patchwork sandwiches

Make sandwiches with sliced pumpernickel and white bread. Trim off the crusts.* Cut the sandwiches into small squares the same size.

Shaped sandwiches

Butter slices of bread. Cut shapes out of them with cookie cutters. Cut the same shapes out of sliced cheese and lay them on the bread.

1 Trim the crusts off sliced white bread.* Spread each slice of bread with cream cheese and lay a slice of ham on top.

2 Roll the slices of bread up lengthwise and wrap them in plastic wrap or tinfoil. Put them in the refrigerator to chill.

3 After two hours, take the rolls out of the refrigerator. Unwrap them and cut them into slices about .5 in (1 cm) thick.

*Ask an adult to help you.

**Be careful with toothpicks – they have sharp points.

SANDWICH BONANZA

And here are the finished sandwiches and rolls with some ideas on how to lay them out on your party table. Arrange small filled rolls to look like a hungry caterpillar wiggling across a plate, complete with legs and antennae. Scatter animal sandwiches on a meadow made from shredded lettuce, and create a patchwork quilt of tiny brown and white sandwiches. Your hungry guests will not know what to eat first!

MUNCHING CATERPILLAR

Cheese and carrot filling

Antennae made from tiny tomatoes on toothpicks

Watercress or Boston lettuce

BUTTERFLY SANDWICH

Sliced tomato and cucumber

Sprouts

Strip of tomato

SAILBOAT ROLLS

Sliced radishes

Sail made from slice of cheese on toothpick

Shredded lettuce

CHEESY PIG SANDWICHES

Egg mayonnaise filling

Legs made from
carrot sticks

Chicken and
mayonnaise
filling

Sliced radishes

Tunafish and
mayonnaise filling

Sliced tomato
and cucumber

Chicken and
mayonnaise filling

Sliced radish
and cucumber

Cheese and
carrot filling

**PATCHWORK
SANDWICHES**

**PINWHEEL
SANDWICHES**

Sandwich made with
white bread

Pumpernickel sandwich

9

CHEESY POTATO BOATS

Stuffed potatoes are a meal in themselves and are easy to make. Here you'll find some unusual ideas on how to decorate them once you have cooked them. Potatoes take a long time to cook, so put them in the oven 1 to 1½ hours before you want to eat them.*

For two people you will need

2 pats of butter

½ cup (50 g) grated cheese

1 large scrubbed potato

For decoration you can use any of these things

Button mushrooms

Strips of cucumber

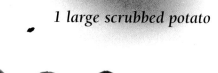

Pitted black olives

Carrots sliced or cut into sticks

COOK'S TOOLS

Small bowl

Knife

Fork

Tablespoon

Grater   *Greased baking sheet*

Sliced cheese cut into shapes

Sliced peppers cut into strips

Shredded lettuce

Watercress

Ask an adult to check if the potatoes are cooked. Leave the oven on for step 3.

Cooking the potatoes

1 Set the oven to 400°F/200°C. Prick the potatoes and place them on the greased baking sheet. Bake for 1¼ hours.*

2 When cooked, cut the potatoes in half lengthwise. Scoop out the middles into the bowl and mash them. Stir in the butter and cheese.

3 Spoon the mixture back into the potato skins and level them off. Then put them back into the oven for another 15 minutes.

*Carefully prick the potatoes using a fork or skewer.

Decorating the potatoes

You can decorate the potatoes once they have been cooked for a second time. Make them into sailboats, ships, or rowboats, as shown here.

SAILBOAT POTATO

Yellow pepper flag

Toothpick mast

Cheese sail

Red pepper deck

POTATO ROWBOAT

Black olives

Carrot oars

Watercress leaves

Cucumber oars

Shredded lettuce for sea

STUFFED SHIP

Watercress steam

Funnels made of sliced carrot and mushroom stalks

Red pepper

SPEEDY PIZZA

This pizza is quick and easy to make.
Here you can see how to make the
pizza and sauce, and on the next
page are some ideas for toppings.
You can make two 4-in (10-cm)
pizzas from the ingredients below.

You will need

A pinch of salt

3 tablespoons butter

3-4 tablespoons milk

*1¼ cups (150 g)
self-rising flour*

*½ cup (50 g)
grated cheese*

1 small onion

*2 teaspoons
tomato paste*

*A pinch each of
salt and pepper*

1 small can tomatoes

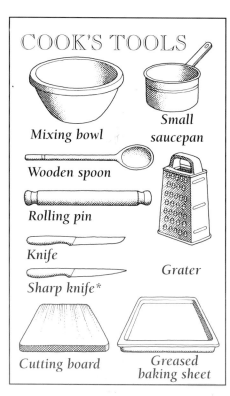

COOK'S TOOLS

Mixing bowl

Small
saucepan

Wooden spoon

Rolling pin

Grater

Knife

Sharp knife*

Cutting board

Greased
baking sheet

Make sure that an adult helps you when you are using a sharp knife.

Making the sauce

1 Set the oven to 425°F/220°C. Peel the onion, then cut it in half and chop it fine on the cutting board.

2 Put the chopped onion in the saucepan. Add the tomatoes, tomato paste, and salt and pepper and stir the mixture together.

3 Cook the mixture over low heat for about 15 minutes, stirring from time to time. Then turn off the heat and let it cool.

Making the dough

1 While the sauce is cooking, make the dough. Put the flour, salt, and butter in the mixing bowl. Cut the butter into small pieces.

2 Rub the pieces of butter into the flour between your fingertips and thumbs until the mixture looks like breadcrumbs.

3 Add the grated cheese and milk to the flour mixture. Mix everything together until you have a smooth ball of dough.

4 Divide the dough in two and make each half into a ball. Roll out each ball into a circular shape about 4 in (10 cm) across.

5 Lay the circles of dough on the greased baking sheet. Spoon the tomato sauce onto them, spreading it evenly to the edges.

6 Decorate the pizzas (see next page). Put them in the oven to cook for 15-20 minutes, until the edges are golden brown.

13

PARTY PIZZAS

If you want, before you cook the basic pizzas you can turn them into something special! Use the ingredients below to try making one of the pizzas shown here, or experiment with ideas of your own.

Grated cheese

Sliced ham cut into strips

Topping ingredients

Pitted black olives

Sliced peppers

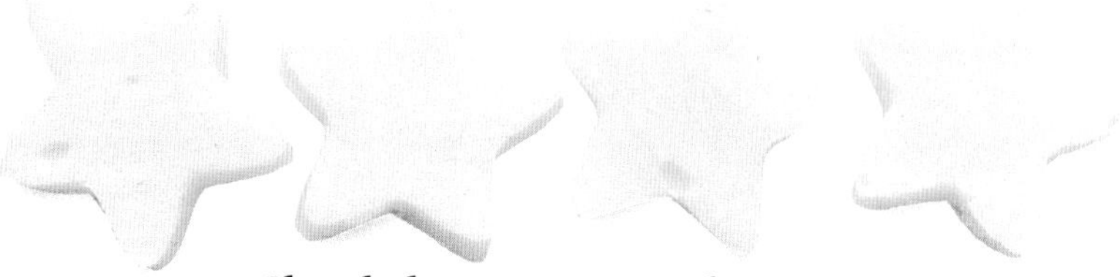

Sliced cheese cut into shapes

Sliced cooked sausage

ITALIAN PIZZA

Chopped red pepper

Sliced cooked sausage

Chopped ham

Sliced mushrooms

Corn

Sliced mushroom

Canned corn

Grated cheese

Chopped green pepper

14

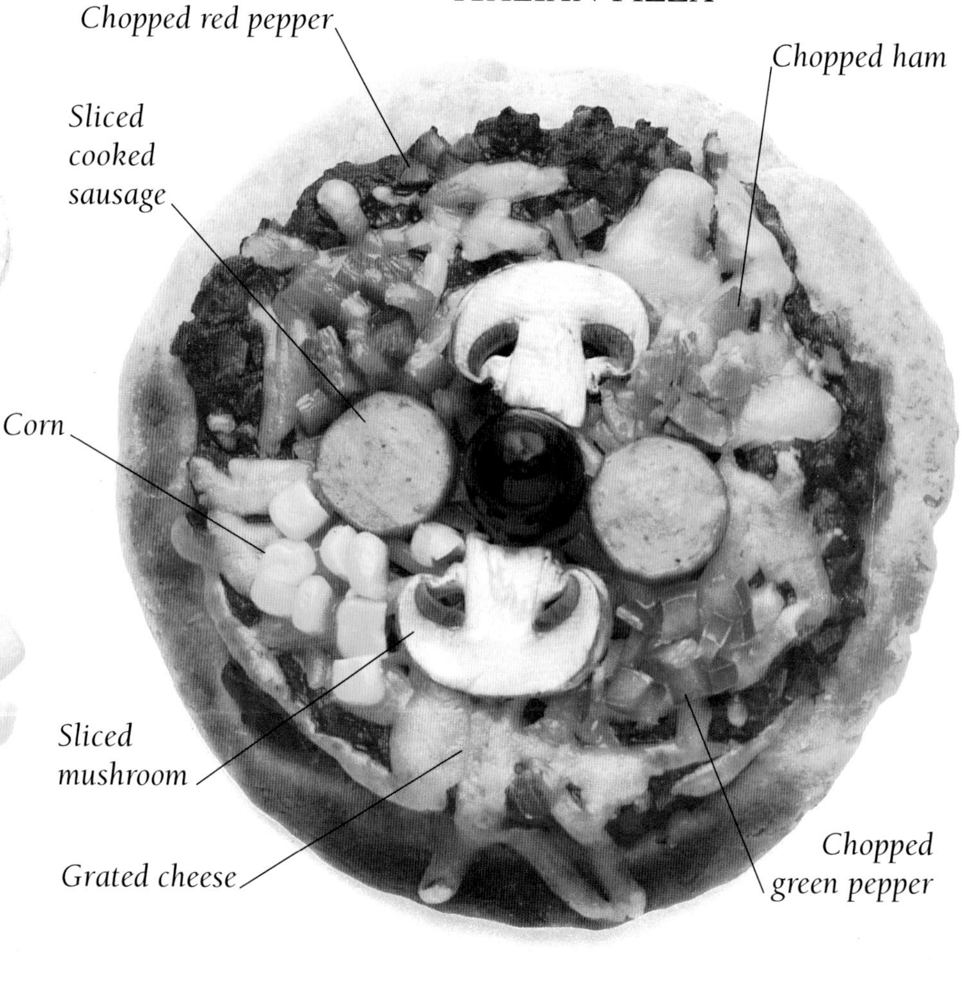

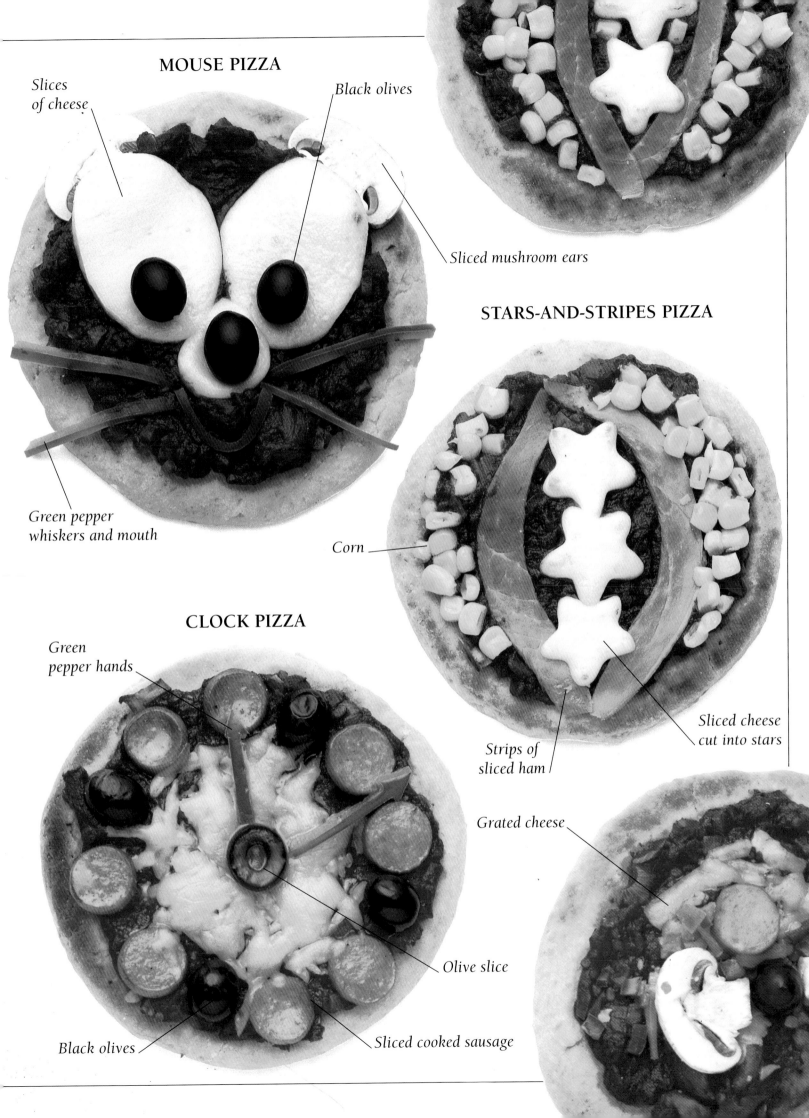

MOUSE PIZZA

Slices
of cheese

Black olives

Sliced mushroom ears

Green pepper
whiskers and mouth

STARS-AND-STRIPES PIZZA

Corn

Sliced cheese
cut into stars

Strips of
sliced ham

CLOCK PIZZA

Green
pepper hands

Olive slice

Black olives

Sliced cooked sausage

Grated cheese

PUFF PASTRY

You can make lots of mouthwatering pastries with ready-made puff pastry. Here you can find out how to make fruity treats, palmiers (palm leaf-shaped pastries), and cheese twists. The ingredients shown are enough to make about thirty pastries.

You will need

1 egg

¼ cup (50 g) light brown sugar (for palmiers)

½ teaspoon white granulated sugar (for fruity treats)

¼ teaspoon ground nutmeg (for fruity treats)

1 tablespoon softened butter (for fruity treats)

12 oz ready-made puff pastry

COOK'S TOOLS

Measuring cup   Baking sheet   Small bowl

4-in (10-cm) plain cookie cutters

Wire rack

Rolling pin

Wooden spoon   Fork

Knife   Pastry brush

1 tablespoon light brown sugar (for fruity treats)

1 heaping tablespoon candied citrus peel (for fruity treats)

*⅓ cup
(25 g)
chopped
roasted hazelnuts
(for palmiers)*

*½ cup (50 g) grated cheddar cheese
(for cheese twists)*

What to do

1 Set the oven to 425°F/220°C. Grease a baking sheet with some butter. Beat the egg in a cup with a fork.

2 Put the pastry on a floured surface and divide it into three equal pieces. You will need one piece of pastry for each recipe.

Fruity treats

1 Roll out the pastry on a floured surface until it is ⅛ in (3 mm) thick. Cut out six circles with the plain cookie cutter.

2 Put the raisins, peel, butter, tablespoon light brown sugar, and nutmeg in a small bowl and mix them together.

3 Put a teaspoon of the mixture in the center of each circle. Brush the circles with egg and pinch the edges together.

4 Turn the bundles over and press them flat. Cut two slits in the top. Brush them with egg and sprinkle white sugar on top.

*⅓ cup (40 g) raisins or
currants (for fruity treats)*

PASTRIES ON PARADE

Hazelnut palmiers

1 Roll the pastry into an 8 x 12 in (20 x 30 cm) rectangle. Brush it with egg and sprinkle on two thirds of the sugar and nuts.

2 Fold the short sides of the rectangle into the middle. Brush them with egg and sprinkle with the rest of the sugar and nuts.

3 Fold the folded edges into the middle. Brush the top with egg. Fold the pastry in half to form a roll. Cut it into 16 slices.*

Cheese twists

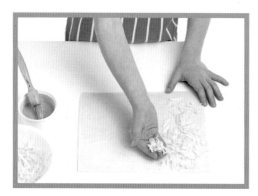  

1 Roll the pastry into an 8 x 10 in (20 x 25 cm) rectangle. Brush it with egg. Sprinkle the cheese over half of the rectangle.

2 Fold the pastry over the cheese to make a sandwich and roll it flat. Trim the edges with a knife.* Brush the sandwich with egg.

3 Cut the sandwich lengthwise into 20 strips.* Twist each strip several times and press the ends onto the baking sheet.

Baking the pastries

Make sure an adult is there to help. Bake the pastries on a greased baking sheet. Cheese twists and palmiers should be baked for 10 minutes and the fruity treats for 15 minutes. The pastries are ready when they are crisp and golden brown. Once they are baked, take them out of the oven and put them on a wire rack to cool. Pastries taste best on the day they are made, so eat them as soon as they are cool!

18 *Ask an adult to help you with any cutting.

The finished pastries

FRUITY TREATS

HAZELNUT PALMIERS

CHEESE TWISTS

19

CHOCOLATE DIPS

You can make delicious homemade chocolate candies by hand-dipping your favorite fruits and nuts. Make candies out of the things shown below and put them in pretty candy cups to give away as presents. You can also use them to decorate a special cake, or, best of all, just enjoy eating them!

You will need

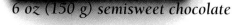

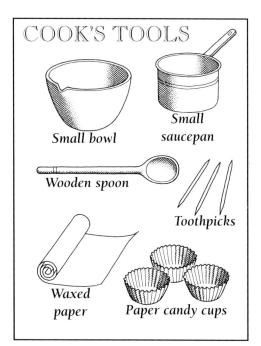

6 oz (150 g) semisweet chocolate

Cherries

Mandarin segments

Brazil nuts

Blanched almonds

Walnuts

COOK'S TOOLS

Small bowl

Small saucepan

Wooden spoon

Toothpicks

Waxed paper

Paper candy cups

Melting the chocolate

1 Break the chocolate up into a bowl. Heat some water in the saucepan over low heat until it just begins to bubble.

2 Set the bowl over the saucepan over low heat. Stir the chocolate with a wooden spoon until it completely melts.

3 Turn off the heat. Very carefully move the saucepan and the bowl from the stove to a trivet or dish towel.

Strawberries

Seedless grapes

Dipping the fruit and nuts

4 One at a time, put a piece of fruit on a toothpick and dip half of it into the chocolate. Then set it on waxed paper to dry.

5 Using your fingers, dip the nuts halfway into the melted chocolate, one at a time. Let them dry on the waxed paper, too.

Arranging your candy

You can put the finished candies in paper candy cups. If they are for a special occasion, arrange them in circular patterns on a large plate.

Punches and Shakes

With the simplest of ingredients you can create wonderful drinks for a party. Below you can find out how to make a basic fruit punch and milkshake. On the next page there are recipes for five mouthwatering "cocktails" on the same theme.

Chocolate drinking powder

Frozen raspberries

You will need

Blackcurrant or grape juice

Honey

Plain yogurt

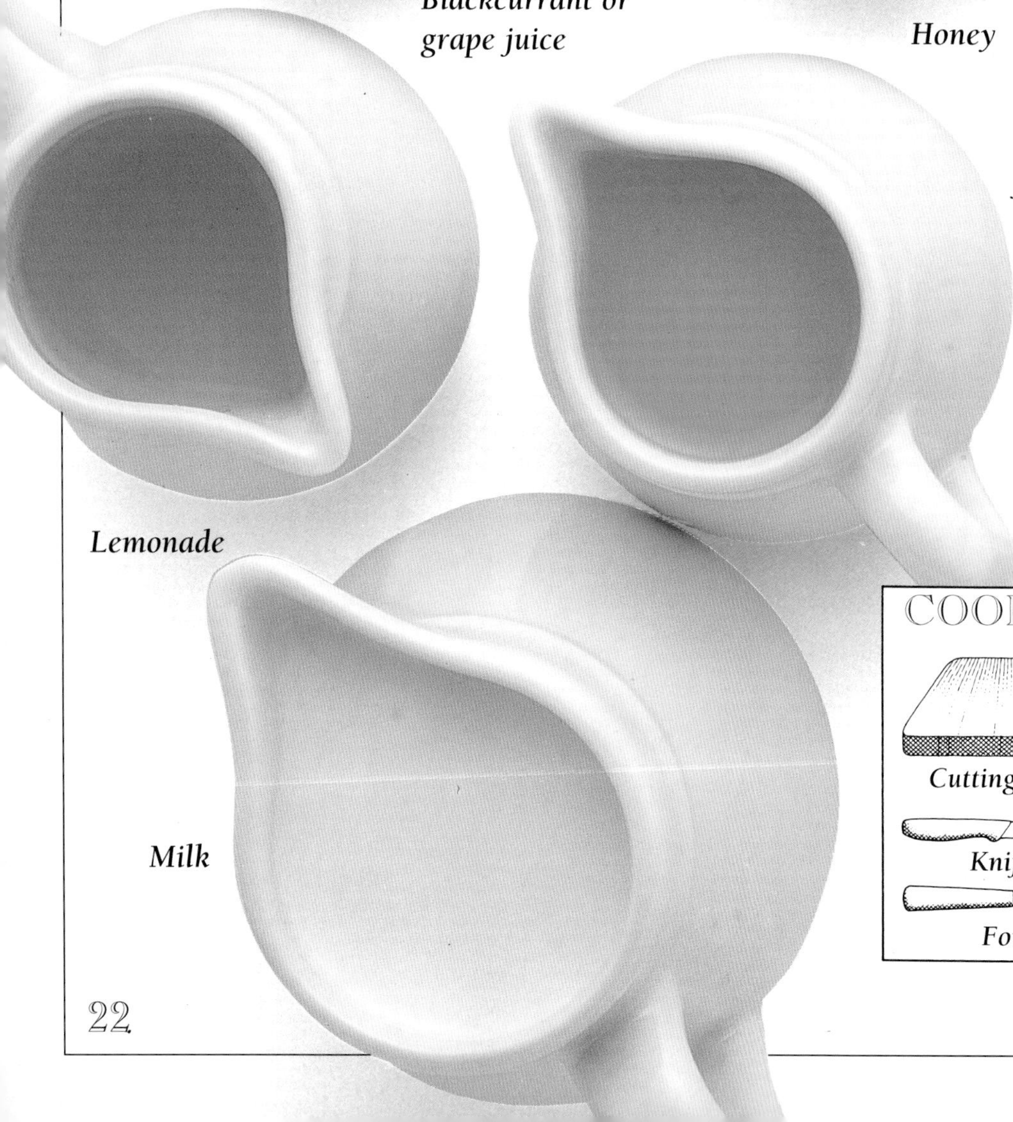

Orange juice

Vanilla ice cream

Lemonade

Milk

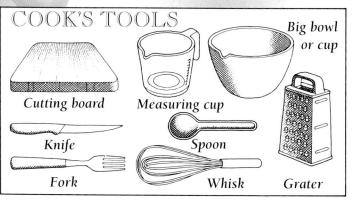

COOK'S TOOLS

Cutting board

Measuring cup

Big bowl or cup

Knife

Spoon

Fork

Whisk

Grater

For decoration

Sliced fruit

Grated chocolate

A banana

Making a fruit punch

1 Wash the fruit you are going to use. Cut it into halves* and take out any pits or seeds, then slice the fruit fine.

2 Put the fruit into a big bowl. Pour orange or grape juice and lemonade over the fruit and gently stir everything together.

Making a milkshake

1 Prepare the fruit you are going to use. Peel and slice bananas.* Take frozen fruit out of the freezer to defrost.

2 Put the fruit in a big bowl and mash it with a fork. You can use a blender to mash the fruit if there is an adult to help you.

3 Add the other ingredients (as listed in the recipes for the drinks on the next page). Mix everything together well.

Ask an adult to help you chop the fruit.

PARTY "COCKTAILS"

And here are five delicious fruit punches and milkshakes based on the recipes shown on the last two pages. Serve them in tall glasses or paper cups and decorate them with sliced fruit and grated chocolate. All the quantities given make drinks for two people, so increase the quantities as necessary.

RASPBERRY FROTH

4 tablespoons raspberries
2 cups milk
2 tablespoons vanilla ice cream
4 tablespoons honey

Follow the milkshake recipe and decorate with a few raspberries.

ORANGES AND LEMONS

1 cup orange juice
1 cup lemonade

Make this like a fruit punch, then slot halved slices of orange around the edge of the glass.

BANANA DREAM

½ cup milk
½ cup yogurt
2 tablespoons vanilla ice cream
1 banana
1 teaspoon honey

Follow the milkshake recipe on page 23 to make the banana dream. Decorate it with slices of banana and kiwi fruit threaded onto a straw.

RUBY FRUIT PUNCH

2 tablespoons blackcurrant
  or grape juice
2 cups lemonade
Sliced apple and nectarine

*Follow the punch recipe to
make the ruby fruit punch.*

CHOCOLATE SHAKE

1 tablespoon chocolate
  drinking powder
2 cups milk
Grated chocolate

*Follow the milkshake recipe,
but mix the chocolate drinking
powder with a little hot water
before adding the milk.
Sprinkle the finished drink
with grated chocolate.*

AMBROSIAS

You can make ambrosias with any fruit soft enough to mash with a fork. Here you can see how to make strawberry or banana ambrosias. The amount of fruit shown for either kind will make four small treats.

You will need

2 tablespoons white granulated sugar

2 small bananas

½ pint (¼ liter) heavy cream or yogurt

A wedge of lemon*

or 2 cups (220 g) strawberries

For decoration

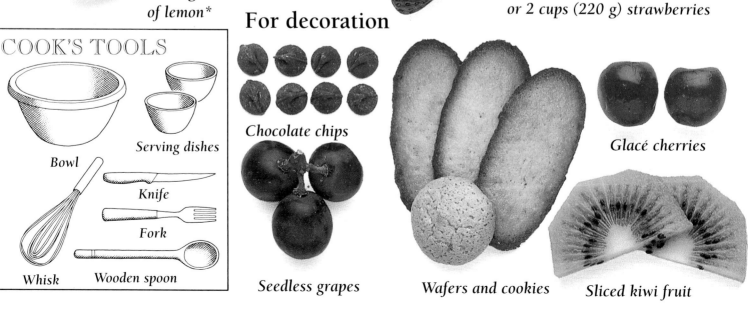

Chocolate chips

Seedless grapes

Wafers and cookies

Glacé cherries

Sliced kiwi fruit

COOK'S TOOLS

Bowl

Serving dishes

Knife

Fork

Whisk

Wooden spoon

26

* A few drops of lemon juice will keep the banana ambrosia from losing its color.

What to do

1 Cut the strawberries in half or peel and slice the bananas.* Put the fruit in the bowl and mash it with a fork until it is smooth.

2 Whisk the cream or yogurt until it is thick and creamy. Add this and the sugar to the mashed fruit. Stir them in well.

3 Pour the fruit mixture into the serving dishes or glasses. Decorate them as shown below, or however you like.

BANANA BEAR

STRAWBERRY DOG

KIWI FLOWER

The banana bear has wafer ears, eyes made of cookies and chocolate chips, a cherry nose, and a slice of kiwi fruit for a mouth.

The strawberry ambrosia dog has sliced strawberry ears, eyes made of grapes, a cookie and chocolate-chip nose, and whiskers made of kiwi fruit.

The flower pattern on this strawberry treat is made of sliced kiwi fruit and glacé cherries arranged around a grape in the middle.

* Ask an adult to help with any cutting. 27

Ice-Cream Sundaes

Ice-cream sundaes are lots of fun to make. All you need is ice cream, some sauces, and lots of tasty things to put on top. You must make sundaes quickly, so that they don't melt. Either put them in the fridge as you finish them, or eat them right away!

COOK'S TOOLS

2 small bowls

Wooden spoon

Knife

Sieve

2 big spoons

Glasses or dishes

Small saucepan

You will need

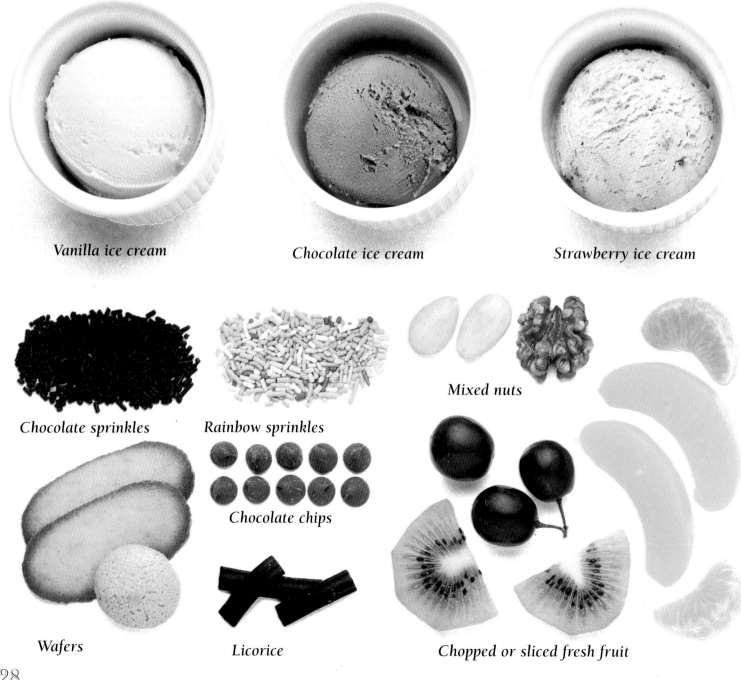

Vanilla ice cream

Chocolate ice cream

Strawberry ice cream

Chocolate sprinkles

Rainbow sprinkles

Mixed nuts

Wafers

Chocolate chips

Licorice

Chopped or sliced fresh fruit

28

Making the sauces

For raspberry sauce

1 cup (150 g) raspberries (frozen or fresh)

⅜ cup (75 g) white granulated sugar

For chocolate sauce

Raspberry sauce

1 Wash the raspberries and put them in a sieve over a bowl. Then push the raspberries through the sieve using a wooden spoon.

2 Add the sugar to the raspberry pulp a little at a time. Then stir the sauce vigorously until all the sugar has dissolved.

4 oz (100 g) semisweet chocolate

Chocolate sauce

1 Break up the chocolate. Put it in the small bowl with the water. Heat some water in the saucepan until it bubbles gently.

2 Place the bowl over the saucepan until the chocolate melts. Turn off the heat and stir the chocolate until smooth.

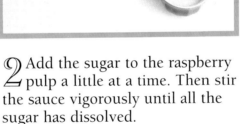

3 tablespoons water

29

SILLY SUNDAES

You can make sundaes that look like colorful insects or flowers by using the ingredients and sauces shown on the last two pages, or experiment with ideas of your own. First put the ice cream in the dishes, then add the sauces and finally the toppings. You will find it easier to scoop ice cream out of containers if you use a metal spoon that you dip into hot water between each scoop.

BUMBLEBEE ICE CREAM

Chocolate sauce

Chocolate-chip eyes

Vanilla ice cream

Wafers

Sliced peaches

BUTTERFLY ICE CREAM

Chocolate-chip eyes

Almonds

Licorice antennae

Sprinkles

Sliced pineapple wings

Chocolate chips

Chocolate ice cream

Grapes

FRUITY FLOWER
(for two people)

Sliced peach

Sliced strawberry

CATERPILLAR ICE CREAM
(for three people)

Use one ball each of chocolate, strawberry, and vanilla ice cream.

Raspberry sauce

Licorice antennae

Cherry nose

Wafer

Chocolate chips

Eyes made of halved grapes

LADYBUG ICE CREAM

Raspberry sauce

Chopped nuts

Sliced kiwi fruit

Strawberry ice cream

Raspberry sauce

Grape eyes

Licorice

Strawberry ice cream

Chocolate-chip spots

31